How Do You Get To School

Written By
Chantay M. Roland

Illustrated By
Terence Flowers

This Book Belongs To

_____

This book is dedicated to all students entering school for the first time.

I wish you the best of luck and continue to grow your mind.

- Chantay

I can ride a car
to school.

I can ride the big yellow bus to school.

I can ride my skateboard to school.

I can ride in a
hot air balloon
to school.

I can ride in a big truck to school.

I can ride on a motorcycle to school.

It does not matter how I get to school as long as I'm here and ready to learn.

Mom, Dad, Auntie, Uncle, Grandma, and Grandpa hurry I can't be late. Hurry please get me to school on time.

Hurry! Hurry! I'm ready to learn.

HOW DO YOU GET TO SCHOOL?

WRITTEN BY
Chantay M. Roland

ILLUSTRATED BY
Terence Flowers

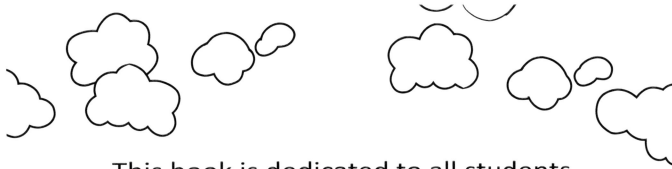

This book is dedicated to all students
entering school for the first time.

I wish you the best of luck and continue
to grow your mind.

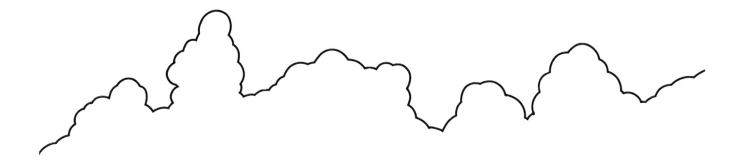

I can ride a car
to school.

I can ride my
skateboard
to school.

I can ride in a big truck to school.

I can ride on a
motorcyle to
school.

Chantay M. Roland is a native of Charlotte, North Carolina, where she attended Charlotte Mecklenburg Schools. She graduated from The University of North Carolina at Charlotte. As a woman, educator, and author, she defines herself as a person striving to fulfill the purpose God created for her. From an early age, she developed a passion for teaching and learning.

Chantay has been molding young minds for over 35 years and has been married to Alvin for 27 years. When she is not teaching, she enjoys reading, writing children's books, traveling, shopping, cooking, attending sporting events, and spending time with her family and friends.

Kindergarten Sight Words

List 1:	List 2:
1. the	21. this
2. a	22. have
3. and	23. from
4. to	24. or
5. in	25. one
6. is	26. had
7. you	27. by
8. it	28. word
9. he	29. but
10. was	30. not
11. for	31. what
12. on	32. some
13. are	33. we
14. as	34. can
15. with	35. out
16. his	36. other
17. they	37. were
18. I	38. all
19. At	39. there
20. be	40. when

Can you find the sight word?

Sample Sentences	Sample Sentences
List 1:	List 2:
The dog ran across the field.	This is my new book.
A cat climbed up the tree.	I have a lot of toys.
I went to the park.	She came from another country.
She wants to go to the store.	Would you like juice or water?
The ball is in the box.	One apple a day keeps the doctor away.
It is a sunny day today.	I had a great time at the party.
You should wash your hands.	The book was written by a famous author.
It is my favorite toy.	Every word in the dictionary has a meaning.
He is playing with his toys.	I like the cake but not the frosting.
She was happy to see her family.	She did not come to school today.

At-Home Sight Word Practice

Sight Word Bingo:

- Create bingo cards with the sight words
- Call out the words and have students cover them on their cards
- First to get 5 in a row wins!

Sight Word Memory/Match:

- Make pairs of sight word cards
- Lay them face down and have students take turns flipping over 2 at a time
- Try to find matching pairs

Sight Word Scavenger Hunt:

- Hide sight word flashcards around the room
- Have students search for and collect the words
- Can time them or have them race against each other

Sight Word Writing Practice:

- Provide students with blank paper or whiteboards
- Call out a sight word and have them practice writing it
- Can time them or have them race against each other

Sight Word Hopscotch:

- Write sight words in the hopscotch squares
- Students take turns tossing a marker and hopping to the word, reading it aloud

Made in the USA
Columbia, SC
22 November 2024

47013620R00015